AuthorHouse™ UK
1663 Liberty Drive
Bloomington, IN 47403 USA
www.authorhouse.co.uk
Phone: 0800 047 8203 (Domestic TFN)
+44 1908 723714 (International)

Because of the dynamic nature of the Internet, any web addresses or links contained in this book may have changed since publication and may no longer be valid. The views expressed in this work are solely those of the author and do not necessarily reflect the views of the publisher, and the publisher hereby disclaims any responsibility for them.

Any people depicted in stock imagery provided by Getty Images are models, and such images are being used for illustrative purposes only.
Certain stock imagery © Getty Images.

This book is printed on acid-free paper.

ISBN: 978-1-7283-5357-9 (SC)
978-1-7283-5356-2 (e)

Print information available on the last page.

Published by AuthorHouse 05/28/2020

authorHOUSE

MESSY JESSIE!

Written by Jack Trott
Illustrated by Mavrodin Cristina

iii

This book is dedicated to
my beautiful daughter
Jessica – Rose

Jessie had lots
of fun playing
with the arts
and crafts

Jessie got covered
in glitter and glue

Teacher replied
"UH HO!
Messy Jessie"

3

On Tuesday jessie went shopping with mummy, however jessie does not like shopping.

4

Jessie was such
a good girl, so
mummy got her
an ice-cream

5

Jessie Ice cream has melted, and she got covered In Ice cream

Mummy replied
"UH OH! Messy Jessie"

On Wednesday jessie goes
to the park with her older
brother to feed the ducks,
as she loves animals

8

Jessie fell in the pond
and SPLASH! Jessie
was soaking wet

10

Brother replied
"UH OH Messy Jessie"

On Thursday Jessie's was

helping daddy paint
her new bedroom

and picked up
a paint brush

Jessie got carried away
with the paint brushes
and got covered in paint

Daddy replied
"UH OH Messy Jessie"

15

On Friday, Jessie loves
to play in the garden

16

She decided she would
play with the flowers

17

The neighbour popped his head over the fence and saw that Jessie was covered in dirt and flowers

The neighbour replied
"UH OH Messy Jessie

On Saturday, Jessie loves to draw with her older sister

This is something they do together while the parents are out

Jessie was making a mess drawing on herself and the walls

Her sister saw she was covered in ink

Sister replied "UH OH Messy Jessie"

23

It was Jessie turn to stir the cake mixture

Jessie made such a mess and got covered in the cake mixture

Grandma replied
"UH OH Messy Jessie

After a long
week of getting
messy, it was
time for Jessie
to have a bath

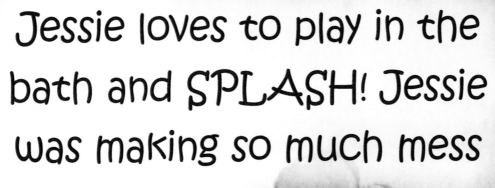

Jessie loves to play in the bath and SPLASH! Jessie was making so much mess

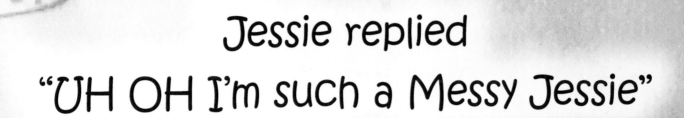

Jessie replied
"UH OH I'm such a Messy Jessie"

31

Lightning Source UK Ltd.
Milton Keynes UK
UKRC012118130620
364867UK00003B/51

* 9 7 8 1 7 2 8 3 5 3 5 7 9 *